The
Happy
Book

1,400 things

FOR KIDS!

to be happy about

The Happy Book by Barbara Ann Kipfer

ILLUSTRATED BY PAUL MEISEL

WORKMAN PUBLISHING, NEW YORK

Library of Congress Cataloging-in-Publication Data
Kipfer, Barbara Ann
1400 things for kids to be happy about/by Barbara Ann Kipfer;
illustrations by Paul Meisel.
p. cm.
ISBN 1-56305-238-5
1. Happiness—Juvenile literature. I. Meisel, Paul, ill.
II. Title. III. Title: Fourteen hundred things for kids to be happy about.
BJ 1481.K55 1994   94-31586
152.4—dc20   CIP
                                                     r94

Workman books are available at special discounts when purchased
in bulk for premiums and sales promotions as well as for
fund-raising or educational use. Special editions or book excerpts
can also be created to specification. For details, contact the
Special Sales Director at the address below.

Workman Publishing Company
708 Broadway
New York, NY 10003

Manufactured in the United States of America

First printing September 1994

10 9 8 7 6 5 4 3

To Kyle and Keir
(and my big "kid", Paul)

THANK YOU

To Peter Workman: for giving me another outlet for my
proliferation of happy thoughts and for kindly
listening to all of my ideas.

To Sally Kovalchick, Lynn Brunelle, and Carbery O'Brien:
for their cheerful editing and support.

To Paul Meisel: for his breathtaking artwork.

And to my sons Kyle and Keir and my husband Paul.
There is no greater happiness than you.

–B.K.

For Peter, Alex, and Andrew

–P.M.

Things to be happy about... me

1. imagination
2. my own thoughts and dreams
3. being happy
4. fingerprints like no one else's
5. my echo
6. doing my best
7. a sense of humor
8. my reflection in a puddle
9. having the answer
10. my "Happy Book"

My List

11. ....
12. ....
13. ....
14. ....
15. ....
16. ....
17. ....
18. ....
19. ....
20. ....

Things to be happy about... my room

21. hats

22. a pet that sleeps with me

23. puzzles

24. secret friends

25. a piggy bank

26. crayons and paints

27. a bucket for my Happy-Meal prizes

28. sunlight

29. my own bookcase

30. toys

My List

31. ....

32. ....

33. ....

34. ....

35. ....

36. ....

37. ....

38. ....

39. ....

40. ....

Things to be happy about... my home

My List

41. ....

42. ....

43. ....

44. ....

45. ....

46. ....

47. ....

48. ....

49. ....

50. ....

51. everything familiar

52. hugs and kisses

53. having a secret hiding place

54. a peg to hang my coat

55. privacy

56. different rooms for different things

57. a warm welcome

58. security

59. family portraits

60. the key under the mat

Things to be happy about ... my backyard

61. visitors at the bird feeder
62. trees to climb
63. lying on the grass to look at stars
64. the doghouse
65. hitting grounders
66. early morning dew
67. hammocks
68. a tree house
69. helping to mow the lawn
70. an outdoor grill

My List

71. ....
72. ....
73. ....
74. ....
75. ....
76. ....
77. ....
78. ....
79. ....
80. ....

Things to be happy about... my family

81. trust

82. jumping on beds

83. smooching parents

84. hand-me-downs

85. traditions

86. built-in playmates

My List

91. ....

92. ....

93. ....

94. ....

95. ....

96. ....

97. ....

98. ....

99. ....

100. ....

87. responsibility

88. reading together

89. making funny faces in the mirror

90. a helping hand

Things to be happy about... my friends

101. sharing

102. nicknames

103. play dates

104. secrets

105. talking on the phone

106. loyalty

107. always saving a place in line

108. sleep-overs

109. inside jokes

110. being a best friend

My List

111. ....

112. ....

113. ....

114. ....

115. ....

116. ....

117. ....

118. ....

119. ....

120. ....

Things to be happy about... pets

121. purrs and tail-wags

122. "fetch"

123. walking the dog

124. a greeting at the front door

125. wet noses and sloppy kisses

126. "WOOF!"

127. feeding the dog under the table

128. pet shows

129. choosing the right name

130. collar tags

My List

131. ....

132. ....

133. ....

134. ....

135. ....

136. ....

137. ....

138. ....

139. ....

140. ....

Things to be happy about... grandparents

141. a cookie jar that's always full

142. being spoiled

143. Grandma's secret recipe

144. looking at old photos together

145. piggyback rides

146. hearing stories about my parents when they were kids

147. getting to stay up late

148. finding neat stuff in a closet

149. antique knickknacks

150. Grandpa's magic tricks

My List

151. ....

152. ....

153. ....

154. ....

155. ....

156. ....

157. ....

158. ....

159. ....

160. ....

Things to be happy about... toys and games

161. tic-tac-toe

162. knowing the punchline of a joke

163. "Go fish!"

164. tongue twisters

165. video games

166. a game of cat's cradle

167. "Simon says..."

168. paper dolls

169. comic books

170. building with blocks

My List

171. ....

172. ....

173. ....

174. ....

175. ....

176. ....

177. ....

178. ....

179. ....

180. ....

Things to be happy about... bedtime

191. bedtime stories

192. the door left open just a crack

193. a soft pillow

194. sweet dreams

195. being tucked in

196. "Don't let the bedbugs bite!"

197. night-lights

198. no monsters in the closet

199. fluffy flannel pj's

200. goodnight kisses

My List

181. ....

182. ....

183. ....

184. ....

185. ....

186. ....

187. ....

188. ....

189. ....

190. ....

Things to be happy about... my body

201. boundless energy

202. goose bumps

203. belly buttons

204. flexing muscles

205. walking, running and tiptoeing

My List

211. ....

212. ....

213. ....

214. ....

215. ....

216. ....

217. ....

218. ....

219. ....

220. ....

206. AH-CHOOOOOOO!

207. brain power

208. funny bones

209. taste buds

210. a cut that heals fast

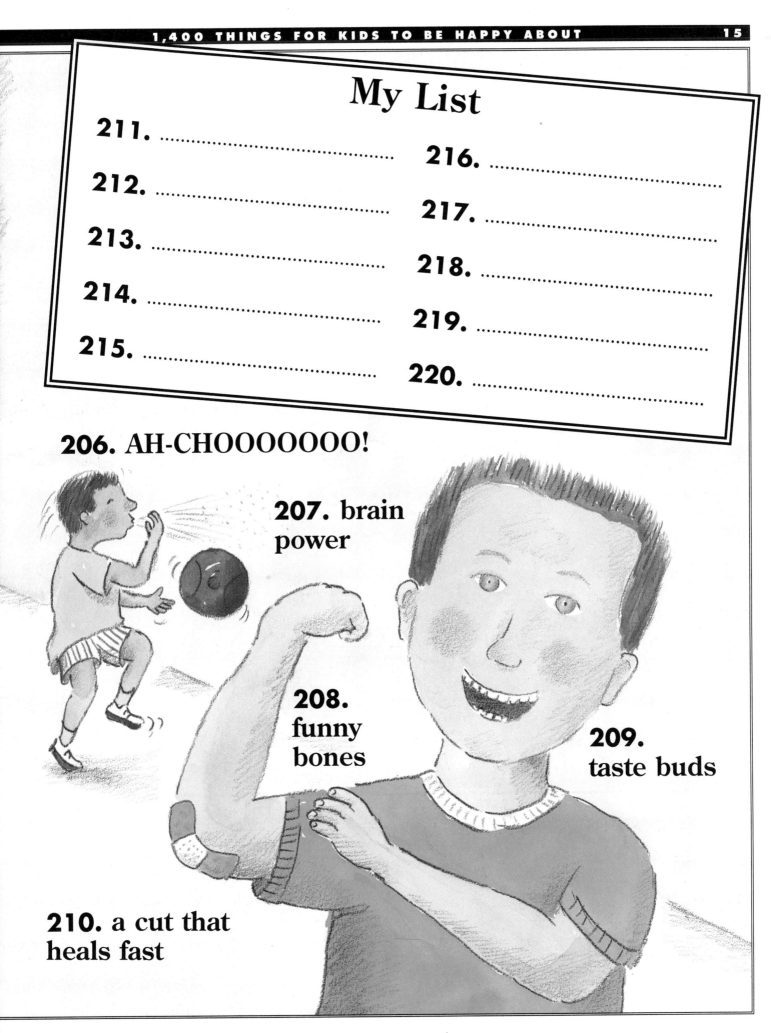

Things to be happy about... in the kitchen

221. cupboards full of good things to eat

222. my own cookbook

223. funny refrigerator magnets

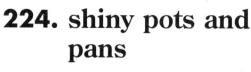

224. shiny pots and pans

225. a bulletin board for special messages

226. being the official taste tester

227. licking the bowl

228. doing homework at the kitchen table

229. a stepping stool to reach high places

230. bare feet on cool tile

My List

231. ....

232. ....

233. ....

234. ....

235. ....

236. ....

237. ....

238. ....

239. ....

240. ....

Things to be happy about... in the garden

251. my own tools

252. the smell of damp earth

253. sprouting seeds

254. roots, fruits and flowers

255. harvesting the crop

256. bugs

257. the sprinkler

258. baby vegetables

259. flowers turning toward the sun

260. having a green thumb

My List

241. ....

242. ....

243. ....

244. ....

245. ....

246. ....

247. ....

248. ....

249. ....

250. ....

Things to be happy about... city neighborhoods

261. tall buildings scrunched together

262. community gardens

263. sirens, horns, whistles

264. hustle and bustle

265. the ice-cream truck

266. Chinese take-out

My List

271. ....

272. ....

273. ....

274. ....

275. ....

276. ....

277. ....

278. ....

279. ....

280. ....

267. block parties and street fairs

268. fire-escape flower pots

269. friendly policemen

270. subways rumbling underground

Things to be happy about... country neighborhoods

291. quiet streets

292. lots of kids who want to play

293. fields to play ball in

294. walking to school

295. secret paths through backyards

296. friendly neighbors

297. baked bean suppers

298. crossing guards who know my name

299. the favorite corner store

300. ponds to explore

My List

281. ....

282. ....

283. ....

284. ....

285. ....

286. ....

287. ....

288. ....

289. ....

290. ....

Things to be happy about... weekends

301. no school

302. the big game

303. wearing comfy old clothes

304. renting a movie

305. free time

306. going out to dinner

307. an extra hour at bedtime

308. Saturday morning cartoons

309. riding my bike

310. miniature golf

My List

311. ....

312. ....

313. ....

314. ....

315. ....

316. ....

317. ....

318. ....

319. ....

320. ....

Things to be happy about... school

My List

321. ....

322. ....

323. ....

324. ....

325. ....

326. ....

327. ....

328. ....

329. ....

330. ....

331. free-choice time

332. a smile from the teacher

333. an "A" on anything

334. artwork on the walls

335. being first in line

336. the class hamster

337. show-and-tell

338. sitting next to my best friend

339. passing notes without getting caught

340. recess!

Things to be happy about... sports

341. playing fair

342. team colors

343. shaking hands with the other team after the game

344. the winning goal

345. cheers from the crowd

346. coaches

347. choosing sides

348. team spirit

349. "2, 4, 6, 8, who do we appreciate!"

350. fun

My List

351. ....

352. ....

353. ....

354. ....

355. ....

356. ....

357. ....

358. ....

359. ....

360. ....

Things to be happy about... studies

361. reading out loud
362. teachers
363. dictionaries
364. making up my own stories
365. fizzy science experiments
366. group projects
367. computer time
368. playing an instrument
369. learning new things
370. what, when, where, why, who, how

My List

371. ....

372. ....

373. ....

374. ....

375. ....

376. ....

377. ....

378. ....

379. ....

380. ....

Things to be happy about... arts and crafts

My List

381. ....

382. ....

383. ....

384. ....

385. ....

386. ....

387. ....

388. ....

389. ....

390. ....

391. cutting out valentines and snowflakes

392. blowing bubbles

393. creating a terrarium

394. being creative

395. face painting

396. candid snapshots

397. homemade rocket ships

398. sock puppets

399. the Crayola jumbo pack

400. potato print Mother's Day cards

Things to be happy about... at the pool

411. the buddy system
412. lifeguards
413. SPLASH!
414. the smell of chlorine
415. "Last one in is a rotten egg!"
416. belly flops
417. playing sharks and minnows
418. dog-paddle races
419. swimming lessons
420. kickboards

My List

401. ....
402. ....
403. ....
404. ....
405. ....
406. ....
407. ....
408. ....
409. ....
410. ....

Things to be happy about... the great outdoors

421. the weather

422. the changing seasons

423. fossil remains

424. birds' nests

425. a sea of grass waving in the wind

426. taking a hike

427. deserts, forests, fields, mountains

428. being out in the open air

429. lots of green underfoot

430. oceans with crashing waves

My List

431. ....

432. ....

433. ....

434. ....

435. ....

436. ....

437. ....

438. ....

439. ....

440. ....

Things to be happy about...
camping

441. counting stars

442. Mother Nature

443. telling ghost stories

444. fellow adventurers

445. toasting marshmallows

446. the fish I caught for dinner

My List

451. ....

452. ....

453. ....

454. ....

455. ....

456. ....

457. ....

458. ....

459. ....

460. ....

447. night visitors

448. zipping up the tent

449. flashlights

450. a warm sleeping bag

Things to be happy about... the animal kingdom

471. animal instincts

472. walking, flying, swimming, crawling

473. zebra stripes

474. kangaroos

475. fur and feathers

476. a rustle in the bushes

477. paw prints

478. whales and dolphins

479. a mother feeding her young

480. roaring, howling, growling

My List

461. ....

462. ....

463. ....

464. ....

465. ....

466. ....

467. ....

468. ....

469. ....

470. ....

Things to be happy about... the plant kingdom

481. grass-blade whistles

482. seeds

483. using sunshine and soil to make food

484. trees

485. sweet-smelling lilacs

486. tall grasses to hide in

487. apple blossoms

488. making leaf rubbings

489. peppermint and other herbs

490. a dandelion fluff explosion

My List

491. ....

492. ....

493. ....

494. ....

495. ....

496. ....

497. ....

498. ....

499. ....

500. ....

Things to be happy about... in the park

501. hot dogs and hamburgers on the grill

502. city skylines

503. starting a new book

My List

511. ....

512. ....

513. ....

514. ....

515. ....

516. ....

517. ....

518. ....

519. ....

520. ....

504. fresh air

505. playing frisbee with
the dog

506. outdoor weddings

507. lemonade
in a thermos

508. no litter

509. wading in
the duck pond

510. remote-
control
sailboats

Things to be happy about...
spring

531. mud

532. being able to ride my bike again

533. Daylight Saving Time

534. robins on the lawn

535. April showers and May flowers

536. no more cold nights

537. warm breezes

538. buds bursting open

539. spring fever

540. baseball opening day

My List

521. ....

522. ....

523. ....

524. ....

525. ....

526. ....

527. ....

528. ....

529. ....

530. ....

Things to be happy about... creepy crawlies

541. looking under rocks

542. an army of ants

543. many-legged centipedes

544. wiggling worms

545. no-see-ums

546. slugs

547. sssssslithering ssssssnakes

548. getting the heebie-jeebies!

549. spiders and beetles

550. *not* getting stung

My List

551. ....

552. ....

553. ....

554. ....

555. ....

556. ....

557. ....

558. ....

559. ....

560. ....

Things to be happy about… fields and woods

My List

561. ....
562. ....
563. ....
564. ....
565. ....
566. ....
567. ....
568. ....
569. ....
570. ....

571. twigs snapping underfoot

572. nuts and berries for animal food

573. finding a perfectly round stone

574. owls hooting and other spooky sounds

575. blazing a trail

576. bat caves

577. secret hideaways

578. natural habitats

579. watching a spider spin its web

580. babbling brooks

Things to be happy about... summer

581. running through the sprinkler
582. berry-picking
583. a swim before supper
584. sunglasses
585. squirt gun battles
586. chasing lightning bugs
587. going barefoot
588. lemonade stands
589. ice cream and popsicles
590. corn on the cob

My List

591. ....
592. ....
593. ....
594. ....
595. ....
596. ....
597. ....
598. ....
599. ....
600. ....

Things to be happy about... the harbor

611. a weathered boardwalk

612. tons of fish

613. ferry rides

614. salty ropes to tie up boats

615. climbing up the spiral stairs of a lighthouse

616. mist

617. lots of boats

618. buoys and gulls

619. fishermen

620. the long blast of a foghorn

My List

601. ....

602. ....

603. ....

604. ....

605. ....

606. ....

607. ....

608. ....

609. ....

610. ....

Things to be happy about... at the beach

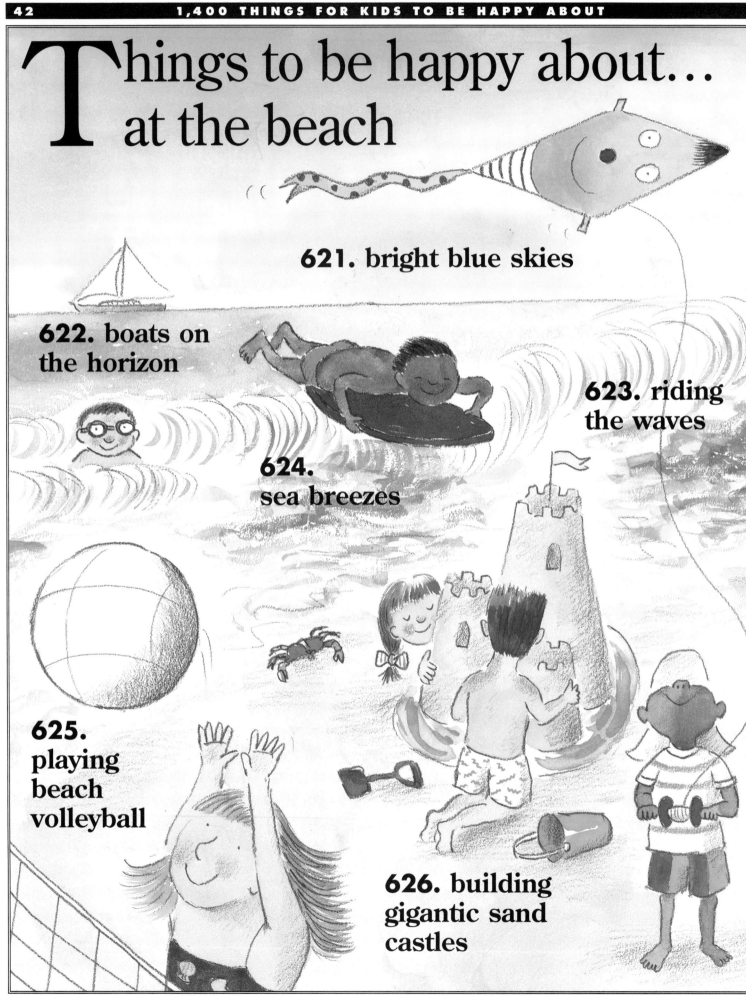

621. bright blue skies

622. boats on the horizon

623. riding the waves

624. sea breezes

625. playing beach volleyball

626. building gigantic sand castles

My List

631. ....

632. ....

633. ....

634. ....

635. ....

636. ....

637. ....

638. ....

639. ....

640. ....

627. friendly seagulls

628. a big blanket that stays put

629. collecting seashells

630. sun hats

Things to be happy about... parades

641. brass bands
642. lining up in expectation
643. banners and flags
644. marching with my troop
645. excitement
646. the Grand Marshal
647. floats
648. booming drums
649. baton twirlers
650. waving to everyone as they pass

My List

651. ....
652. ....
653. ....
654. ....
655. ....
656. ....
657. ....
658. ....
659. ....
660. ....

TROOP 95

Things to be happy about... on the 4th of July

671. red, white and blue

672. "Yankee Doodle"

673. cookouts

674. "The Star-Spangled Banner"

675. freedom

676. spectacular fireworks

677. 1776

678. pride and patriotism

679. The Declaration of Independence

680. our flag

My List

661. ....

662. ....

663. ....

664. ....

665. ....

666. ....

667. ....

668. ....

669. ....

670. ....

Things to be happy about... tastes

681. salty tears

682. sour apples

683. a cheeseburger and fries

684. a fresh tomato from the garden

685. the sea

686. watermelon

687. thick milkshakes

688. licking a stamp

689. spicy salsa

690. gooey hot-fudge sundaes

My List

691. ....

692. ....

693. ....

694. ....

695. ....

696. ....

697. ....

698. ....

699. ....

700. ....

Things to be happy about... colors

701. different eye colors

702. blushing

703. the rainbow

704. a grape-juice mustache

705. yellow rain slickers

706. red bricks

707. bluebirds

708. the blue-green ocean

709. silver coins

710. faded blue jeans

My List

711. ....

712. ....

713. ....

714. ....

715. ....

716. ....

717. ....

718. ....

719. ....

720. ....

Things to be happy about... farms and ranches

721. funny scarecrows

722. dungarees

723. planting seeds for the very first time

My List

731. ....

732. ....

733. ....

734. ....

735. ....

736. ....

737. ....

738. ....

739. ....

740. ....

724. milking the cow

725. the smell of hay

726. sitting on fences

727. oinks, grunts and other pig noises

728. a pet horse

729. "cock-a-doodle-doo!!!"

730. feeding the baby chicks

Things to be happy about…smells

741. freshly mowed grass

742. bread right out of the oven

743. roses

744. the gas station

745. a wet dog

746. dinner

747. clean laundry

748. bacon sizzling

749. scratch-and-sniff books

750. bubble gum

My List

751. ....

752. ....

753. ....

754. ....

755. ....

756. ....

757. ....

758. ....

759. ....

760. ....

Things to be happy about... sounds

761. wind chimes

762. laughter

763. a roaring crowd

764. sparrows chirping

765. waves lapping against the shore

766. a happy baby

767. the crack of a baseball against a bat

768. whistling for the first time

769. my own heartbeat— "lub dub, lub dub"

770. music, music, music

My List

771. ....

772. ....

773. ....

774. ....

775. ....

776. ....

777. ....

778. ....

779. ....

780. ....

Things to be happy about... fall

781. new notebooks and pencil cases

782. spectacular sunsets

783. sweater weather

784. jumping into a big pile of leaves

785. pumpkin patches and apple orchards

My List

791. ....

792. ....

793. ....

794. ....

795. ....

796. ....

797. ....

798. ....

799. ....

800. ....

786. hayrides

787. talking with the wind

788. the first day of school

SCHOOL

789. carving pumpkins

790. autumn colors

APPLE CIDER

Things to be happy about... the country fair

801. farm animals all together

802. a fiddling concert

803. pony rides

804. patchwork quilts

805. raffles

806. enormous pumpkins and squashes

807. blue ribbons

808. corn dog stands

809. the shot that wins the prize

810. entering a pie eating contest

My List

811. ....

812. ....

813. ....

814. ....

815. ....

816. ....

817. ....

818. ....

819. ....

820. ....

Things to be happy about... our country

821. land of opportunity

822. The President of the United States

823. The Pledge of Allegiance

824. national parks

825. the Liberty Bell

826. 50 states

827. the founding fathers

828. "From Sea to Shining Sea"

829. the melting pot

830. exploring space

My List

831. ....

832. ....

833. ....

834. ....

835. ....

836. ....

837. ....

838. ....

839. ....

840. ....

Things to be happy about...
Halloween

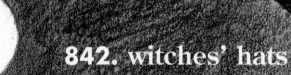

841. "BOO!"

842. witches' hats

843. grinning
jack-o-lanterns

My List

851. ....

852. ....

853. ....

854. ....

855. ....

856. ....

857. ....

858. ....

859. ....

860. ....

844. ghosts and goblins

845. scary masks

846. candy corn

847. making my own costume

848. trick-or-treat

849. real black cats

850. funny teeth

Things to be happy about... make believe

871. fighting fire-breathing dragons

872. playing house

873. dressing up the cat

874. "Let's pretend..."

875. clowning around

876. fancy tea parties

877. being a fairy princess at the ball

878. fantasy

879. swashbuckling

880. Peter Pan

My List

861. ....

862. ....

863. ....

864. ....

865. ....

866. ....

867. ....

868. ....

869. ....

870. ....

Things to be happy about... wishes and dreams

881. world peace
882. living in another time period
883. meeting a sports hero
884. being a movie star
885. flying
886. a trip to outer space
887. being president
888. exploring a new land
889. discovering treasure
890. curing all diseases

My List

891. ....
892. ....
893. ....
894. ....
895. ....
896. ....
897. ....
898. ....
899. ....
900. ....

Things to be happy about... Thanksgiving

911. Pilgrims and Native Americans

912. leftovers

913. pumpkin pie

914. feeling stuffed

915. watching football on TV

916. giving thanks

917. wishing on a wishbone

918. late-night cold turkey sandwiches

919. family stories and laughter

920. roast turkey with stuffing

My List

901. ....

902. ....

903. ....

904. ....

905. ....

906. ....

907. ....

908. ....

909. ....

910. ....

Things to be happy about... winter

921. catching snowflakes on my tongue

922. a new sled

923. icicles

924. woolly socks

925. frozen ponds to skate on

926. foggy-breath clouds

927. a mug of steamy hot chocolate

928. frosty-window finger drawings

929. putting out birdseed

930. making a snow angel

My List

931. ....

932. ....

933. ....

934. ....

935. ....

936. ....

937. ....

938. ....

939. ....

940. ....

Things to be happy about... holidays

941. Santa Claus

My list
puppy
mitt
puzzles
bike
skates

942. Peace on Earth

943. counting the days

For Santa

944. stockings hung from the mantel

My List

951. ....

952. ....

953. ....

954. ....

955. ....

956. ....

957. ....

958. ....

959. ....

960. ....

945. the star on top of the Christmas tree

946. all the trimmings

947. tying a red bow on the dog

948. hunting for Easter eggs

949. lighting candles

950. Dad proudly carving the turkey

Things to be happy about... traveling

971. meeting the pilot

972. singing in the back seat

973. "Are we there yet?"

974. reading road signs

975. the clickety-clack of the train

976. flying above the clouds

977. maps

978. packing my own suitcase

979. buckling up

980. tunnels and bridges

My List

961. ....

962. ....

963. ....

964. ....

965. ....

966. ....

967. ....

968. ....

969. ....

970. ....

Things to be happy about... vacation

981. staying in a hotel

982. souvenirs

983. my very own passport

984. tasting new food

985. exploring

986. making new friends

987. keeping a journal

988. snapping photos

989. writing postcards home

990. sightseeing

My List

991. ....

992. ....

993. ....

994. ....

995. ....

996. ....

997. ....

998. ....

999. ....

1,000. ....

Things to be happy about... colonial times

1,001. the land of plenty

1,002. Paul Revere

1,003. early settlers

1,004. log cabins

1,005. cooking supper in the fireplace

1,006. the *Mayflower*

1,007. 13 colonies

1,008. powdered wigs and hoop skirts

1,009. trailblazers

1,010. the first Thanksgiving

My List

1,011. ....

1,012. ....

1,013. ....

1,014. ....

1,015. ....

1,016. ....

1,017. ....

1,018. ....

1,019. ....

1,020. ....

Things to be happy about... the old west

1,021. ghost towns

1,022. wide-open spaces

1,023. pueblos

1,024. the Pony Express

1,025. GOLD!

1,026. cowboys

1,027. adventurous pioneers

1,028. chuck wagons

1,029. herds of buffalo

1,030. tumbling tumbleweed

My List

1,031. ....

1,032. ....

1,033. ....

1,034. ....

1,035. ....

1,036. ....

1,037. ....

1,038. ....

1,039. ....

1,040. ....

Things to be happy about... museums

My List

1,041. ....

1,042. ....

1,043. ....

1,044. ....

1,045. ....

1,046. ....

1,047. ....

1,048. ....

1,049. ....

1,050. ....

1,051. Native American artifacts

1,052. Egyptian mummies

1,053. the museum gift shop

1,054. a real suit of armor

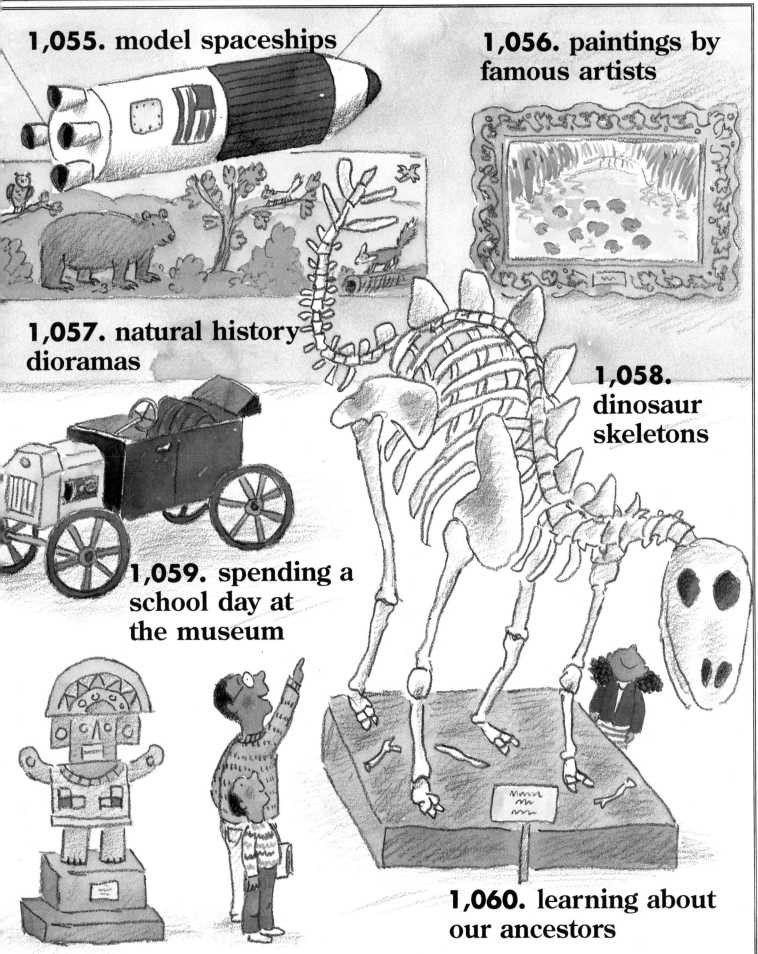

1,055. model spaceships

1,056. paintings by famous artists

1,057. natural history dioramas

1,058. dinosaur skeletons

1,059. spending a school day at the museum

1,060. learning about our ancestors

Things to be happy about... in the sky

1,061. fluffy white clouds

1,062. planes that leave trails

1,063. leaves blowing

1,064. birds soaring

1,065. fog

1,066. hot-air balloons

1,067. lightning and thunder

1,068. pop flies

1,069. high-flying kites

1,070. swooping swallows

My List

1,071. ....

1,072. ....

1,073. ....

1,074. ....

1,075. ....

1,076. ....

1,077. ....

1,078. ....

1,079. ....

1,080. ....

Things to be happy about... outer space

1,081. astronauts

1,082. stars, stars, stars

1,083. eclipses

1,084. the man in the moon

1,085. finding the Big Dipper

1,086. looking through a telescope

1,087. the Milky Way

1,088. Saturn's rings

1,089. shooting stars

1,090. rockets and satellites

My List

1,091. ....

1,092. ....

1,093. ....

1,094. ....

1,095. ....

1,096. ....

1,097. ....

1,098. ....

1,099. ....

1,100. ....

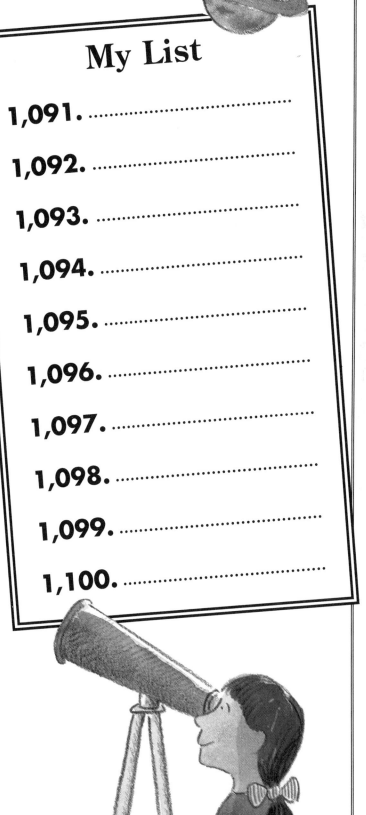

Things to be happy about... rainy days

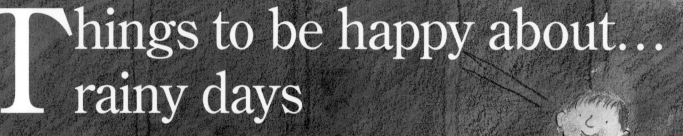

1,101. playing dress-up

1,102. checking for rainbows

1,103. a new computer game

1,104. beating Dad at Monopoly

1,105. being cozy

1,106. putting on a puppet show

1,107. the sound of rain on the roof

1,108. finding treasures in the attic

My List

1,111. ....

1,112. ....

1,113. ....

1,114. ....

1,115. ....

1,116. ....

1,117. ....

1,118. ....

1,119. ....

1,120. ....

1,109. building a model ship

1,110. sleeping in

Things to be happy about... the library

1,131. comfy chairs

1,132. borrowing any book I want

1,133. big tables to spread out at

1,134. reading programs

1,135. my own library card

1,136. stacks and stacks of books

1,137. helpful librarians

1,138. Shhhh!

1,139. reading silently

1,140. story hour

My List

1,121. ....

1,122. ....

1,123. ....

1,124. ....

1,125. ....

1,126. ....

1,127. ....

1,128. ....

1,129. ....

1,130. ....

Things to be happy about... TV

1,141. world news

1,142. VCRs

1,143. favorite reruns

1,144. armchair travels

1,145. learning new things

1,146. the remote control

1,147. TV dinners

1,148. game shows

1,149. funny commercials

1,150. a couch I can stretch out on

My List

1,151. ....

1,152. ....

1,153. ....

1,154. ....

1,155. ....

1,156. ....

1,157. ....

1,158. ....

1,159. ....

1,160. ....

Things to be happy about... the supermarket

My List

1,161. ....

1,162. ....

1,163. ....

1,164. ....

1,165. ....

1,166. ....

1,167. ....

1,168. ....

1,169. ....

1,170. ....

1,171. the deli counter

1,172. a treat

1,173. a cool store on a hot day

1,174. pushing the cart

1,175. unloading the groceries

1,176. exotic foods

1,177. picking out a new cereal

1,178. automatic doors

1,179. wide aisles

1,180. the lobster tank

Things to be happy about… at the movies or a play

1,191. a giant bucket of popcorn

1,192. going with a friend

1,193. sneak previews

1,194. pretending I'm the hero as I leave the theater

1,195. a red velvet curtain

1,196. seeing the actors after the show

1,197. soft seats

1,198. a double feature

1,199. applause

1,200. curtain calls

My List

1,181. ....

1,182. ....

1,183. ....

1,184. ....

1,185. ....

1,186. ....

1,187. ....

1,188. ....

1,189. ....

1,190. ....

Things to be happy about... the playground

1,201. TAG!

1,202. not being IT

1,203. swings that go really high

1,204. double Dutch

1,205. picking teams for dodgeball

1,206. the big slide

1,207. getting silly

1,208. "One potato, two potato…"

1,209. a hiding place to tell secrets

1,210. jungle gyms

My List

1,211. ....

1,212. ....

1,213. ....

1,214. ....

1,215. ....

1,216. ....

1,217. ....

1,218. ....

1,219. ....

1,220. ....

Things to be happy about... doctors and dentists

1,231. first aid

1,232. medicine to make you better

1,233. clean teeth

1,234. the little rubber hammer that tests reflexes

1,235. games in the waiting room

1,236. friendly doctors

1,237. warm stethoscopes

1,238. no shots!

1,239. saying "AAAAH"

1,240. a healthy checkup

My List

1,221. ....

1,222. ....

1,223. ....

1,224. ....

1,225. ....

1,226. ....

1,227. ....

1,228. ....

1,229. ....

1,230. ....

Things to be happy about... firehouses

1,241. safety first

1,242. the brass pole

1,243. sirens

1,244. polishing the shiny red engine

1,245. ladders

1,246. the captain's big hat

1,247. winding up hoses

1,248. dalmatians

1,249. pictures of old-time horse-drawn fire trucks

1,250. big black boots

My List

1,251. ....

1,252. ....

1,253. ....

1,254. ....

1,255. ....

1,256. ....

1,257. ....

1,258. ....

1,259. ....

1,260. ....

Things to be happy about... amusement parks

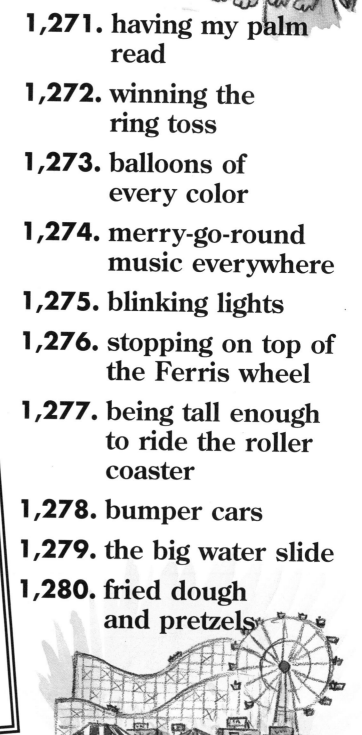

1,271. having my palm read

1,272. winning the ring toss

1,273. balloons of every color

1,274. merry-go-round music everywhere

1,275. blinking lights

1,276. stopping on top of the Ferris wheel

1,277. being tall enough to ride the roller coaster

1,278. bumper cars

1,279. the big water slide

1,280. fried dough and pretzels

My List

1,261. ....

1,262. ....

1,263. ....

1,264. ....

1,265. ....

1,266. ....

1,267. ....

1,268. ....

1,269. ....

1,270. ....

Things to be happy about... the circus

1,281. trapeze artists flying through the air

1,282. highwire balancing

1,283. three rings

1,284. the ringmaster in top hat

1,285. crunching on peanuts and candied apples

1,286. clowns in huge shoes

1,287. the menagerie

1,288. acrobats

1,289. the strong man

1,290. the big top

My List

1,291. ....

1,292. ....

1,293. ....

1,294. ....

1,295. ....

1,296. ....

1,297. ....

1,298. ....

1,299. ....

1,300. ....

Things to be happy about... parties

My List

1,301. ....

1,302. ....

1,303. ....

1,304. ....

1,305. ....

1,306. ....

1,307. ....

1,308. ....

1,309. ....

1,310. ....

1,311. silly hats and noisemakers

1,312. clown magicians

1,313. lots of presents

1,314. breaking the piñata

1,315. party games

1,316. the giggles

1,317. surprises

1,318. yummy snacks

1,319. being the guest of honor

1,320. icing on the cake

Things to be happy about... music

1,321. jazz

1,322. "Row, row, row your boat"

1,323. clapping to the beat

1,324. harmony

1,325. dancing wildly

1,326. crashing cymbals

1,327. kazoos

1,328. "Do-re-mi-fa-so-la-ti-do"

1,329. the conductor waving his wand

1,330. Christmas carols

My List

1,331. ....

1,332. ....

1,333. ....

1,334. ....

1,335. ....

1,336. ....

1,337. ....

1,338. ....

1,339. ....

1,340. ....

Things to be happy about... eating out

1,341. drawing on placemats

1,342. being waited on

1,343. pizza

1,344. sitting in a booth

1,345. a juke box

1,346. cherries in my soda

1,347. mints when I leave

1,348. no dishes to do

1,349. ordering what I want

1,350. fancy desserts

My List

1,351. ....

1,352. ....

1,353. ....

1,354. ....

1,355. ....

1,356. ....

1,357. ....

1,358. ....

1,359. ....

1,360. ....

Things to be happy about... the zoo

1,361. a yawning hippo

1,362. feeding time at the seal tank

1,363. strutting peacocks

1,364. cotton candy and caramel popcorn

1,365. bears napping in the sun

1,366. monkeys acting just like people

1,367. the long neck of a giraffe

1,368. tweets, roars, groans, squeals

1,369. animals I've never seen before

1,370. penguins in tuxedos

My List

1,371. ....

1,372. ....

1,373. ....

1,374. ....

1,375. ....

1,376. ....

1,377. ....

1,378. ....

1,379. ....

1,380. ....

Things to be happy about... saving the earth

1,391. recycling

1,392. making a compost pile

1,393. solar power

1,394. planting a tree

1,395. using recycled paper

1,396. riding my bike instead of riding in a car

1,397. picking up litter

1,398. adopting an animal at the zoo

1,399. showers instead of baths

1,400. thinking green

My List

1,381. ....

1,382. ....

1,383. ....

1,384. ....

1,385. ....

1,386. ....

1,387. ....

1,388. ....

1,389. ....

1,390. ....